Devotions from the Garden

Inspiration for Life

Candee Fick

DEDICATION

This devotional is dedicated to my maternal grandfather who was passionate about organic gardening. If only I'd inherited more of your green thumb.

CONTENTS

The following collection of devotional readings was inspired by previous blog posts at *Encouragement for the Journey* (now found at www.CandeeFick.com).

INTRODUCTION

As I write this, it's summertime. Day after long day of hot temperatures, afternoon thunderstorms, mosquitoes, picnics in the park, swimming pools, and fresh vegetables from the garden. But the bounty on the table didn't happen by accident. The ground was prepared and seeds planted. Watering, weeding, and thinning took up more time as we waited for the first varieties to ripen. And later this fall, we'll be busy canning and freezing the harvest to carry us through the long, cold winter ahead. Then, once we start to see the first signs of spring, the cycle will repeat itself.

I have found that life is like a garden, too. Complete with seasons of dormancy and growth, preparation and harvest. A winter, spring, summer, and fall of the soul.

WALKING IN THE GARDEN

"Since we live by the Spirit, let us keep in step with the Spirit." ~ Galatians 5:25

For the past five summers, our family has exchanged our time share condo and spent a week in Branson, Missouri. In addition to boating on and swimming in Table Rock Lake, we get passes to Silver Dollar City. Wrapped in and around the amusement park rides, shows, and shops are a lush variety of plants lining the pathways. I know that the higher humidity and lower altitude play a big role in producing such bounty, but that didn't stop me from pausing to admire the colorful foliage and flowers surrounded by tall shade trees.

It reminded me of a time during my college days in Tulsa, Oklahoma. Just months before graduation, I discovered a garden-like park hidden away in a neighborhood near where I was student-teaching.

2

Paths wound between bushes and flowerbeds all in bloom. Overhead, trees bore new leaves and birds filled the air with singing as sweet as the aroma of spring blossoms.

The garden beckoned and I longed to spend hours meandering to explore every corner. If only there had been a special someone to walk with hand-in-hand, sharing our dreams and whispering the secrets of our hearts. Simply walking and talking in the garden in the cool of the day.

Yet, there was. And still is.

Because God longs to spend time with me. He wants to walk around with me through every day. Just like back in the Garden of Eden, He comes "walking in the garden of the cool of the day" (Genesis 3:8). It's up to me whether I will come out of hiding and keep in step with Him.

A family vacation at a crowded amusement park reminded me of how much I long to spend time walking in the garden with God. I wonder which path we'll take and what we'll talk about today.

What about you? Do you have a favorite place to walk? Do you walk with God through all of life or only select portions?

SPRING CLEANING

"'I am the true vine, and my Father is the gardener. He cuts off every branch in me that bears no fruit, while every branch that does bear fruit he prunes so that it will be even more fruitful. '" ~ John 15:1-2

The calendar said that Spring officially started a couple of weeks ago, but we happened to be blessed with a snow day from school just three days later. That's Colorado weather for you. At least this time, the snowdrifts melted within days instead of weeks.

Once I could finally see my poor flower beds again, I was more than ready for Spring to really arrive. Warmer weather stirred my anticipation but there was a little something I needed to take care of first. A little something I didn't quite get to last fall when I should have. Sigh.

It's time to clean out the dead growth and matted leaves in my flower bed. Time to prune the rosebushes. Time to pick the windblown litter off the thorns and out of the rocks. All to make room for new growth to happen and to allow air and water to get to the plants. Not to mention it makes the place look well-tended instead of neglected.

Kinda like the rest of my life. It's time for a little Spring cleaning. So, I'm making room for new growth and opportunities by cutting wasted time and otherwise "good" activities that take time away from my family. Digging out old roots of bitterness and unforgiveness. Throwing away feelings of rejection and inadequacy. Dusting off neglected ideas.

Because Spring is coming to my heart. I want to be ready to see what God has in store.

What about you? What are you cleaning out of your neglected areas? What are you hoping to grow there instead?

GREENING UP

"Forget the former things; do not dwell on the past. See, I am doing a new thing! Now it springs up; do you not perceive it? I am making a way in the desert and streams in the wasteland." ~ Isaiah 43:18-19

Once I cleaned out the flower beds, I discovered something. Something green. Something growing under all the dead stuff. My hyacinth bulbs were peeking through the dirt and I would have missed them.

I moved on to the row of rosebushes and spotted that green color again. At the base of each bush, green was creeping upward as if the plant was slowly waking up.

Everywhere I turned, things were greening up. From the hints of my favorite color scattered through the dry brown grass of the lawn to the tiny buds swelling on the tree branches. New life was emerging after the cold, dark winter.

What about in my heart? Do I see evidence of new growth in my own life? Am I dead and dry? Or is the sap of God's love flowing through me? As I feed my soul -- just like my yard gets sunshine, fresh air, and water -- I should start to see life springing up in the once barren wastelands.

Winter may have been long and bitterly cold, but Spring is on the way.

What about you? Have you felt the drain of Winter? Are you growing something new this season? Is it Spring in your heart? How can you tell?

BLOOMING

"See! The winter is past; the rains are over and gone. Flowers appear on the earth; the season of singing has come, the cooing of doves is heart in our land. The fig tree forms its early fruit; the blossoming vines spread their fragrance." ~ Song of Songs 2:11-13a

Something amazing happens in the Spring. Grass turns green. Trees get new leaves.

And the bulbs I buried in the dirt send up green leaves and a stalk stretching for the sky. Atop each, a bud forms and grows until it shows a hint of the color within. And, seemingly overnight, the flowers in my yard unfurl their petals in an explosion of color and fragrance. Hyacinths and daffodils. Tulips and lilies. Followed by the lilac bush and cherry blossoms. And the roses. Oh, the roses.

It's a celebration long in the making.

Kinda like my life. I'm a wife, a mother, a legal researcher, a Bible study leader, a singer, a friend, and a writer. Each area is quietly growing behind the scenes and underground. And then green shoots reach heavenward and buds form. My personal garden blooms in ways I could only have imagined during the dark days of winter when nothing seemed to be happening.

For example, while I might be in the winter as a writer, slowly pounding out and polishing words in private, hints of spring are emerging. Positive comments from critique partners. Queries and proposals in the mail. Articles and manuscripts under consideration. Invitations to judge contests. Mentoring other writers. Slowly the buds of hope grow.

Spring is coming and someday my personal garden will bloom anew.

What about you? What is growing in your garden? Is anything blooming?

PLANTING

"A man reaps what he sows. The one who sows to please his sinful nature, from that nature will reap destruction; the one who sows to please the Spirit, from the Spirit will reap eternal life." ~ Galatians 6:7b-8

"Don't judge each day by the harvest you reap, but by the seeds you plant." ~ Robert Louis Stevenson

Now that my flower beds are ready, my fingers are itching for the garden. But I live in Colorado and it's too early to plant anything outside. (Way too early since it's been known to snow around here in mid-May.)

Does that mean I'm out of luck? No. There's plenty to do right now.

First, I plan. How big will the garden be? What varieties of vegetables and how many of each? (Definitely make sure there isn't too much zucchini!)

Second, I get the seeds. Planning to plant doesn't mean a thing unless I have the raw materials on hand when the day arrives.

Third, while it's too early to plant outdoors, I can still start seedlings inside. I still remember trips to my grandparents' house and seeing my grandfather's greenhouse with rows of milk cartons, each with a tiny green shoot poking up through the dirt.

What lessons can I learn from planting?

I need to identify what crop I want to grow in my life. Love. Joy. Patience. Compassion. Friendships. Faith. Spiritual growth. Ministry. Publication.

Knowing the expected harvest, tells me what kind of seeds to plant. Because "a man reaps what he sows." Just like I can't get corn from a tomato seed, I can't grow compassion on a root of jealousy. I can't plant hours of television time and expect a book to get written. I can't expect my faith to grow without planting time in the Word and in prayer.

And I need to get started. Even if the weather isn't quite right outside for my tiny seedling to survive, I can still begin within a sheltered environment.

What about you? What seeds are you planting in your life? What harvest do you expect from them?

TILLING

"When a farmer plows for planting, does he plow continually? Does he keep on breaking up and harrowing the soil? When he has leveled the surface, does he not sow ...?" ~ Isaiah 28:24-25a

While our selected seeds are sprouting indoors, it is time to prepare the soil outside. Time to fire up the Rototiller or pick up a shovel.

It's time to turn the ground over. To break up the big chunks. To stir organic material into the natural clay. To loosen the dirt so that future plant roots have room to grow and that air and water can circulate.

My life sometimes needs the same upheaval. Otherwise I risk becoming hard and the new growth I desire is stunted.

So how do I till my life? Through change. By trying a

new routine or adopting a fresh outlook on an old habit. I shake things up again, even if only for a season. Read a book by a new author. Turn the dial to a new radio station. Take a different route home. Try a new recipe or restaurant. Explore a different genre of writing.

What about you? Is there an area of your life that's needs tilling? How?

COMPOSTING

"And we know that in all things God works for the good of those who love him, who have been called according to his purpose." ~ Romans 8:28

Part of preparing the soil of our garden includes adding organic material to the soil. And nothing beats the "black gold" of compost.

Compost. That mixture of decaying organic matter, such as leaves and manure, that is used as fertilizer. Where else can trash like used coffee grounds, banana peels, shredded newspaper, and grass clippings be transformed into something vitally useful? Into something that will feed my plants the nutrition they need and result in a bigger harvest.

Quality compost material doesn't happen overnight. It takes heat and time to transform the rotting garbage into a rich growing material.

What about my life? Given enough time, even my old mistakes and disappointments can be transformed into rich material. Material to feed additional growth in my life and nutrition to add to the lives of those around me.

Take for example my being an extremely shy introvert in junior high and high school. I felt the pain of being a wallflower. The insecurity of not having close friends. The awkwardness of wanting to say something yet being afraid of rejection.

Bottom line? Those were years I'd rather forget. Until I walk into a room today and see someone acting just like I used to. My social mistakes as a teen have taught me how to reach out to the people around me. And how to cultivate quality relationships. Now that's compost at its finest.

What else is compost in my life? Words I wish I could take back have taught me sensitivity and tact. Opportunities I wish I would have taken have given me the courage to take risks. First drafts of stories that will never see the light of day have given me experience and fed my passion for writing.

What about you? Have any of your past experiences been transformed into growing material? Has that compost enriched the lives of others?

HARDENING OFF

"When Pharaoh let the people go, God did not lead them on the road through the Philistine country, though that was shorter. For God said, 'If they face war, they might change their minds and return to Egypt.' So God led the people around by the desert road toward the Red Sea." ~ Exodus 13:17-18a

Once you've got your seedlings started and the soil prepared, it's still not quite time to put the plants in the ground. Not only do you have to wait for the weather to warm up (especially here in Colorado), but the baby plants need a period of hardening off before they can survive the harsh world.

Young and fragile plants raised in the protected environment of a greenhouse can go into shock when exposed to the real world. They need to adapt and acclimate to their new surroundings through increasing periods of exposure to the outdoor conditions. This gradual process thickens the surface of the leaves and prevents excess loss of water later.

What's that got to do with my life?

Well, some of my dreams (like my writing) are fragile seedlings. And if I launch them into the world before they are ready, they may wither and die when exposed to the harsh red pen of editors. So, I expose my ego and writing gradually. A writing group here. A critique partner there. A conference appointment. A contest. My skin gets thicker and I can withstand the winds of correction and criticism.

It reminds me of a story in the Bible when God delivered the Children of Israel out of slavery in Egypt. Instead of leading them along the shortest path to the Promised Land, God led them the long way through the wilderness. Why? Because they would face war on the other path. And facing difficulties so soon might make them turn back instead of go forward.

What about you? Do you have fragile dreams or thin skin in areas? What can you do to "harden off" the seedlings so they can survive the elements of life?

WATERING

"He will be like rain falling on a mown field, like showers watering the earth." ~Psalm 72:6

April showers bring May flowers. Or so I heard back in Elementary school.

What's that got to do with growing a garden? Well, in addition to having nutrient-rich soil in a sunny spot, you need water. And not just water on the surface, but deep down where the roots will eventually spread out. Whether it comes as a sprinkling or a downpour, consistent rain is necessary to prevent long-term drought.

When the rain comes, do we welcome the rain or complain about it ruining our picnic plans? Do we huddle under umbrellas or splash in the puddles? Do we find the sound of rain on the rooftop soothing or irritating?

Life also brings times of rain. And it is just as necessary to our personal growth. But, when it comes, do we let the refreshing moisture soak into our souls? Or does it run off the hardened clay of our hearts? Do I resent the cloudy days or learn to be thankful in the middle of storms?

After all, *"life isn't about waiting for the storms to pass, but learning to dance in the rain."* ~ Unknown

What about you? Is there rain in your life? How are you responding?

PROTECTING

"And the peace of God, which transcends all understanding, will guard your hearts and your minds in Christ Jesus." ~ Philippians 4:7

Ever read the book about Peter Rabbit? That mischievous bunny just couldn't resist the lure of Mr. McGregor's garden. Lettuce, carrots, beans, radishes. A feast worth crawling under a gate for. All until he got chased around by an angry gardener with a rake.

Part of gardening involves putting up some type of barrier to protect the plants from outside invaders - ranging from children's (and dog's) trampling feet to deer to birds to insects. Wise gardeners put up fences and cover fruit trees with nets. They may choose to thwart the bad bugs with insecticides, friendly bugs, or by planting hairy vetch beside the potatoes. (Something my dad told me about last week.)

But what about my life? How do I guard my heart against the invaders of worry and fear? Do I let the insects of doubt eat away at my faith? Or do I erect a wall of truth? Cover myself with hope? Grow patience and gentleness and joy?

One of my favorite passages in the Bible is found in the book of Philippians. ***"Do not be anxious about anything, but in everything, by prayer and petition, with thanksgiving, present your requests to God. And the peace of God, which transcends all understanding, will guard your hearts and minds in Christ Jesus."***

Did you see that word buried in there? Guard. As in being kept by a garrison. Surrounded by a moat. Hidden away inside an army fortress. Protected.

What about you? What tries to invade your life and steal your fruitfulness? What is guarding your heart and mind? How do you know?

WEEDING

"Search me, O God, and know my heart; test me and know my anxious thoughts. See if there is any offensive way in me, and lead me in the way everlasting." ~ Psalm 139: 23-24

With rich, nutritious soil and enough water and sunshine, what grows in my garden? Very hardy weeds, that's what.

Although my youngest son loves to pick the pretty yellow flowers, I'm destined to crawl around on my hands and knees trying to get to the roots and make sure they never show their mocking faces in my garden or yard again. Whether I use a hoe or a hand spade, I am on a mission to get rid of the weeds before they take over. Week after week, I wage war. (And don't get me started on the insidious bind weed that strangles and drags down previously healthy plants.)

What about in my life? Do I have weeds? Those activities that compete for my time and energy and space? Emotions that wrap me up in a tangle of bitterness and resentment? Attitudes of materialism or envy that crop up only to mock my peace?

And am I as diligent in weeding out (pardon the pun) my life as I am my yard? Do I dig deep to expose the roots? Or do I relax my vigilance and let them creep back in? Do I ask God to point out the areas that need work?

What about you? Are there weeds in your life? How do you identify them? And how do you get rid of them?

THINNING

"'Everything is permissible' —but not everything is beneficial. 'Everything is permissible' —but not everything is constructive." ~ 1 Corinthians 10:23

The hardest aspect of gardening for me is the thinning. Why should I pull up perfectly good carrot or cucumber plants? And why pinch blossoms off pumpkin and watermelon vines? It's not like they're weeds.

But, if I leave too many plants in a small area, none of them will grow to their full potential. They'll compete for nutrients and space. And a single vine can't put energy into a dozen melons. By thinning the rows and pinching blossoms, I allow my garden to maximize the resources for the greatest yield.

I face the same problem in my own life. While I can set up protective barriers and yank up the weeds, I have a difficult time saying "No" to good activities. There's nothing wrong with singing in the choir, leading a Bible study, working a part-time job, writing a novel, driving my kids to various activities, scrapbooking, exercising, and doing yard work. Unless I'm stretched so thin that I have to shortchange one area to juggle the next. Or skip sleep, which is never a good idea.

It's time to do a little thinning. Even the "good" must make way for the "best" in my life. So, I'm doing a lot of praying for wisdom and re-evaluating the seasons of my life. For example, choir and Bible study are about to take a break for the summer while the yard work is picking up. So, maybe the summer would be a good time to catch up on my scrapbook. Or simply a time to relax with the kids by the swimming pool, spend time in the Word, and recharge my creative well.

What about you? Do you have a hard time saying "No?" What needs to be thinned from your schedule?

AWARE OF THE UNSEEN

"Still others, like the seed sown among thorns, hear the word; but the worries of this life, the deceitfulness of wealth and the desires for other things come in and choke the word, making it unfruitful." ~ Mark 4:18-19

While working in my yard this summer, I discovered again the insidious nature of the un-cared-for areas of life. All because of some raspberries and an Ash tree.

Six years ago, we planted several raspberry plants along our back fence along with a bed of strawberries, two cherry trees and a couple grapevines. (We enjoy our homemade jams and jellies!) The front yard got an Autumn Purple Ash tree, surrounded by a bed of bulbs and perennials.

Fast forward to last summer when the raspberries really started taking over. New shoots cropped up everywhere, but they were manageable. Mostly in the right spots, even if they were annoying (and prickly) when harvesting the strawberries, cherries and grapes. I meant to corral them ... but never quite got around to it.

Until this summer.

Instead of gallons of fresh strawberries in early June, we harvested one small bowl. The raspberries were choking them out and blocking the sunshine. Not only that, the cherry trees had whole sections without blossoms because they were being surrounded. Oh, and did I mention that baby raspberry plants were cropping up in the middle of the lawn?

What once was a small problem had become a major chore and took hours of work to dig up. And in the process, I discovered the cherry trees had sent up suckers last year. But they'd been hidden behind the raspberries and required a handsaw to cut them off at the ground.

Meanwhile, the bulbs in my front yard bloomed beautifully. The tree did not. I waited and waited, checking the ends of each twig for buds. Nothing. My neighbors all had leaves, but we didn't. Because of a little ash borer bug (and his friends) who'd been living inside the trunk of our tree and destroying it from the inside out. I didn't even know there was a problem until all that was left was a dry, cracked, and lifeless shell of a tree.

So, because I hadn't paid attention to the trunk or known that I should spray for bugs, we got to dig up the Ash tree and all of the surrounding bulbs and plants. And then plant a new tree. And new plants. And new mulch. And I'll need to get new bulbs this fall.

The lessons I've learned? Pay attention to the little things. Take care of them early. And be aware of what's going on under the surface - where unwelcome bugs and roots spread with destructive consequences.

What about you? Are you aware of what's growing under the surface of your life? How do you take care of those areas?

FLIGHT OF THE BUMBLEBEE

"Jesus replied, 'What is impossible with men is possible with God.'" ~ Luke 18:27

Ever watch a bumblebee fly? Tiny wings carry their relatively large bodies from flower to flower.

According to folklore, bumblebees aren't supposed to be able to fly. Someone somewhere did a few simple calculations and determined that it is impossible for a bumblebee to remain airborne according to the laws of aerodynamics.

Tell that to the bumblebee.

Nowadays, more sophisticated analysis shows that bumblebees can fly because their wings operate more like helicopter blades. Plus, their muscles vibrate rather than expand and contract. This allows them to beat their wings 10 to 20 times faster than if they relied on nerve firing impulses alone.

So, you're asking, what does a bug found in the garden have to do with life?

Has anyone ever said that it is "impossible" to achieve a certain dream? Have you looked at the available facts, added up the pros and cons, and determined the goal is out of reach? Yet, is there something hidden within - something others can't see - that will propel us into the future?

Then maybe we're more like bumblebees than we once thought.

What about you? What dreams are you pursuing despite the arguments to the contrary?

CATERPILLARS AND BUTTERFLIES

"Do not conform any longer to the pattern of this world, but be transformed by the renewing of your mind." ~ Romans 12:2a

This journey called life changes us. Sometimes through heat, pressure, irritation, or being broken. But other times, we end up waiting in the dark for something to happen.

Kinda like butterflies in the garden.

This insect starts out as a worm, er, caterpillar. It spends its days crawling around and eating. As it grows, it sheds its old skin for a new one. While it might have interesting stripes and fuzzy hair, the caterpillar is anchored to the ground by gravity.

Then, one day, the caterpillar spins a cocoon and disappears. Literally. For a long time. While inside, the caterpillar's tissue is broken down and a new structure is formed. This is the transformation stage.

At last, the shell is broken open and a butterfly emerges. Fragile, colorful wings are unfurled and tested in the breeze. Until, at last, the insect takes flight for the rest of its life. Soaring and migrating to places it never imagined as a caterpillar.

What about me? Yep, some days I feel like a worm. Anchored down by responsibilities. I might have a few semi-attractive characteristics but, really, all I do I live for me and my needs. (And, I'll stop before I mention growing and, um, needing to get some new skin, er, clothes.)

Then comes a time of transformation. Often in the dark since I can't see what God is doing. Waiting and waiting for something to happen. Yet, I'm being changed from the inside out. I'm a little cramped and can't wait to get out of this place. It's uncomfortable.

Finally, I feel myself breaking free. Seeing the light after so much darkness. Spreading wings I didn't know I had. Gaining altitude and a new perspective. Going places I'd only dreamed of.

What about you? What stage of this process are you in? Does knowing there's a butterfly at the end make the waiting worthwhile?

HUMMINGBIRDS

"As the deer pants for streams of water, so my soul pants for you, O God. My soul thirsts for God, for the living God. When can I go and meet with God?"
~ Psalm 42:1-2

Growing up, I remember seeing a hummingbird feeder and watching these tiny birds fly by for a drink. With wings beating furiously, they hovered near the red pseudo-flowers for mere moments before flitting away.

Then I learned a little bit about hummingbirds. Not only are they really small, they flap their wings an average of 55 times per second (depending on the species) and can even fly backwards. With all this activity, it's no wonder they must consume up to twice their body weight in nectar and small bugs every day.

I also discovered that hummingbirds spend about 80% of their time perching and resting. Why? Because they live on the edge of their energy envelope and flying burns a lot of calories. I learned they eat almost constantly because they live three hours from death. They live on the brink of dying.

What about my life? Granted, my physical metabolism is far from hummingbird-level and I shudder to imagine eating a hundred-something pounds of food every day. But my spiritual and emotional metabolism? It seems like I can burn though my reserves with a single hectic school morning.

That's why, like the hummingbird, I must feed daily on the Word of God and be filled with His Spirit. Feed daily as though I am on the edge of starvation. Feed daily so I can live.

Where do I get my nourishment? Some comes in chunks of time reading my Bible, listening to worship music in my car, or praying while exercising on the treadmill. Other times, I feed in brief snatches. A whispered prayer, a verse taped to my mirror, a glimpse of creation that calls to my soul.

What about you? Do you have hummingbirds where you live? How is your spiritual or emotional metabolism? How often do you need to feed? Do you live like you're dying?

HARVESTING

"Let us not become weary in doing good, for at the proper time we will reap a harvest if we do not give up." ~ Galatians 6:9

No series about gardening would be complete without discussing the final product.

After months of preparing, planting, watering, weeding, thinning ... and waiting in anticipation, the first vegetables are finally ready. Baskets and bowls of sugar snap peas, radishes, carrots and lettuce are transformed into salads even kids will eat. Fresh corn on the cob and yellow summer squash. Cucumbers in vinegar water and stuffed zucchini boats. And salsa from fresh-picked tomatoes, onions, garlic, jalapenos, and cilantro. Don't forget the fall with pumpkins to carve and seeds to roast.

Harvesting. Washing. Eating. Enjoying. Canning. Freezing. Sharing (especially that extra zucchini).

What about me? I've stirred up the rocky places of my life and let God turn my failures into rich compost. I've found good seeds to plant and been diligent to protect, weed, and thin the growth. I've done what I can do. The rest is up to God. While I wait, He causes the seeds to grow into healthy plants, capable of bearing a plentiful harvest.

What's growing in the garden of my life? Faith. A solid marriage. The mentoring of three children. Financial stability (i.e. dwindling debt). Two novels (plus articles, a children's book, a non-fiction book for parents with special-needs children, and devotional book ideas). And I can hardly wait to see the full harvest.

What about you? What's growing in your garden? Are you enjoying the fruit of your labor or still waiting for the harvest?

BLOOMING IN WINTER

"The desert and the parched land will be glad; the wilderness will rejoice and blossom. Like the crocus, it will burst into bloom; it will rejoice greatly and shout for joy." ~ Isaiah 35:1-2a

At the end of every growing season, there comes a time of dormancy. When the leaves turn colors and fall to the ground. When we heap mulch over delicate roots to protect them from the coming cold. When Fall turns into Winter with shorter days, freezing temperatures, and piles of snow.

Yet, in the middle of dark days, hope still blooms. Case in point? The Christmas Cactus.

I have one of these unique plants. A gift from the members of a Bible study I led, the green foil wrapped pot found a new home near my kitchen sink. Days after bringing it home, the lone bloom dropped.

Christmas came and went without a glimpse of color.

Well, any color besides green.

Green leaves sprouted new green leaves. I watered weekly. I turned the pot so the cactus got an even distribution of sunlight. And I wondered if it was worth the work. I mean, how many blooms would I get? One? Three? Five? After a year's waiting, would that make it worth the effort?

Winter faded into Spring and outside my flowerbeds came alive with tulips and daffodils. Summer burst onto the scene with roses and strawberries. Months passed and the chrysanthemums added their color to the yard. Leaves changed colors and fell to the ground as Fall gave way to snowstorms.

And inside, the cactus stayed green.

Then, months later on a snowy day, I caught a glimpse of a different color. A tiny bump of pink on the tip of a green leaf. A closer inspection found more of them. As the buds grew, so did my anticipation.

Until one day, they opened. Large blooms of deep pink at the end of November.

A timely reminder that hope still blooms in the middle of darkness. That Spring will come again.

DEAR READER

I hope you enjoyed exploring a few life lessons from gardening.

Please consider writing an online review to tell others about your favorite life lesson as illustrated through gardening. You can also check out my bonus Pinterest board dedicated to gardening tips.

If you liked these lessons about faith and life illustrated through the gardening, you might also like Book Two in the *Creation Declares* series. *Be Like a Tree: The Keys to a Fruitful Life* is a longer devotional focused on topics like growing tall, hindrances to growth, branching out, and bearing fruit using a variety of trees as examples.

Last, but not least, be the first to know about new releases and special offers by signing up for my author newsletter at www.CandeeFick.com. New subscribers are entered in a drawing for an Amazon gift card and are often surprised with a free book!

Thanks for reading!

Candee

ABOUT THE AUTHOR

Candee Fick is the wife of a high school football coach and the mother of three children including a daughter with a rare genetic syndrome. When not busy with her day job or writing, she can be found cheering on the home team at football, basketball, baseball, and Special Olympics games. In what little free time remains, she enjoys exploring the great Colorado outdoors, indulging in dark chocolate, and savoring happily-ever-after endings through a good book.

She has published articles and non-fiction books while continuing to polish her novel-writing craft. She is a member of American Christian Fiction Writers and speaks to various groups about writing, faith, and facing challenges as a mother. In addition to her blog, Candee can be found on Twitter, Facebook, and Pinterest. (See her website at www.CandeeFick.com for links, to follow her blog, or sign up for newsletter updates.)

MORE BOOKS BY THIS AUTHOR

Be Like a Tree: The Keys to a Fruitful Life (2013) ~ Collection of devotional readings inspired by Psalms 1 and Jeremiah 17. You too can be like a tree firmly planted and nourished beside the waters. Available in print and e-book formats.

Making Lemonade: Parents Transforming Special Needs (2011) ~ Strategies and encouragement for parents raising kids with developmental, behavioral, and/or health needs. Available in print and e-book formats.

Pigskin Parables: Devotions from the Game of Football (2011) ~ Collection of short devotions inspired by previous blog posts. Available in print and e-book formats.

Pigskin Parables: Exploring Faith and Football (2012) ~ An eleven-week devotional including more lessons of faith and life illustrated on the football field. Available in print and e-book formats.

Made in the USA
Monee, IL
03 August 2023

40443100R00028